Digest of the
New Testament

Digest of the
New Testament

BY
DR. TOM WALLACE

SWORD of the LORD PUBLISHERS
Post Office Box 1099 • Murfreesboro, Tennessee 37133

All Scripture quotations are from
the King James Bible.

Printed and Bound in the United States of America

Contents

Preface

This New Testament survey material was gathered, compiled and presented to a large adult Sunday school class over a period of twenty-seven weeks. It proved to be a rewarding and profitable experience for teacher and pupil alike.

The regularity of attendance, the steady increase of interest and obvious spiritual growth of the students gave evidence of the value of these lessons.

This short digest is intended to serve as a foundation for studying the New Testament books in depth. It is hoped that the bird's-eye view will save the student valuable hours of time that may be invested in further in-depth study.

THE GOSPEL OF MATTHEW
The King of the Jews

KEY VERSES: Matthew 23:37–39

"O Jerusalem, Jerusalem, thou that killest the prophets, and stonest them which are sent unto thee, how often would I have gathered thy children together, even as a hen gathereth her chickens under her wings, and ye would not!

"Behold, your house is left unto you desolate.

"For I say unto you, Ye shall not see me henceforth, till ye shall say, Blessed is he that cometh in the name of the Lord."

KEY WORDS

"Kingdom of heaven"—used 33 times
   1st use: chap. 3:1, 2
   Most significant use: chap. 3:1, 2
"Fulfilled"—used 16 times
   1st use: chap. 1:22
   Most significant use: chap. 26:56

THEME

1. To show that Jesus is the Messiah
2. To reveal Him as Prince (chaps. 1–12), Prophet (chaps. 13–23), Priest (chaps. 24–28)

1

3. To explain Jesus' relationship to two great covenants
   a. The Abrahamic covenant of promise (Gen. 15:18)
   b. The Davidic covenant of kingship (II Sam. 7:8–16)

DATE
A.D. 37

WRITER
Matthew (called Levi—Mark 2:14)
   Son of Alphaeus
   A Jew from Galilee; Roman tax collector (Matt. 9:9)

WRITTEN
To: Jews (65 references to the O.T.)
From: Judea

THE BOOK
Number in Bible	40
Number in N.T.	1
Chapters	28
Verses	1,071

PURPOSE
1. To show that the Lord of the Christian is the Messiah of the Jew
2. To show that Jesus of Nazareth is the prophesied King of Israel

DIVISIONS
Five famous discourses in Matthew, chapters 5–24
1. Teacher and His pupils: chaps. 5–7
2. Master and His servants: chap. 10
3. King and His subjects: chap. 13
4. Head of the church and His members: chaps. 16–18

2

5. Judge and His defendants: chap. 24

OUTLINE
I. Preparation for His Public Ministry: Chapters 1–4
   A. Genealogy: chap. 1:1–17
   B. Birth: chaps. 1:18–2:23
   C. Introduction and baptism: chap. 3
   D. Temptation: chap. 4
II. Precepts of His Ministry: Chapters 5–7
   A. Eight rules for living
   B. Formula for happiness
   C. Standard of perfect human conduct
   D. An octave of kingdom music
   E. Eight-rung ladder to radiance and joy
   F. Proclamations of the King
   G. Theme—righteousness
   H. Magna Carta of the kingdom
   I. Platform of the millennium
   J. Spirit will accept; flesh will reject
III. Power of His Ministry: Chapters 8–12
   A. Power over disease, nature and Satan: chap. 8
   B. Power over sin, death and darkness: chap. 9
   C. Power in lives of disciples—past, present, future: chap. 10
   D. Power in life of John the Baptist: chap. 11
   E. Power of Satan and sin: chap. 12
IV. Principles of His Ministry: Chapters 13–15
   A. Parables setting forth kingdom truth: chap. 13
   B. Provision for His followers: chap. 14
   C. Prophets opposed to His ministry: chap. 15
V. Presentation of His Ministry: Chapters 16–23
   A. Great testimony of Peter: chap. 16

    B. Glorious transfiguration: chap. 17

    C. Grand truth of church and kingdom: chap. 18

    D. Good teaching of Christ on divorce and riches: chap. 19

    E. Great tale of parable of laborers: chap. 20

    F. Gallant triumphant entry: chap. 21

    G. Guarded tribute question: chap. 22

    H. Ghastly trouble pronounced on false teachers: chap. 23

VI. Passion of His Ministry: Chapters 24–28

    A. He will return in power and great glory: chap. 24.

    B. He will judge the nations: chap. 25.

    C. He is denied and betrayed: chap. 26.

    D. He is tried and crucified: chap. 27.

    E. He is resurrected, then commissions His disciples: chap. 28.

MISCELLANEOUS

About Matthew: Chapters 9–10

1. Call to apostleship: chap. 9:9

2. Change of profession: chap. 9:9

3. Charge by Jesus: chap. 9:37–38

4. Channeling to service: chap. 10:1–7

THE GOSPEL OF MARK
The Servant of Man

KEY VERSE: Mark 10:45

"For even the Son of man came not to be ministered unto, but to minister, and to give his life a ransom for many."

KEY WORDS
"Straightway"—used 19 times
1st use: chap. 1:10
Most significant use: chap. 1:18
"Immediately"—used 17 times
1st use: chap. 1:12
Most significant use: chap. 10:52

THEME
Jesus Christ is presented as the suffering Servant

DATE
A.D. 50–55

WRITER
John Mark
Cousin of Barnabas: Col. 4:10
Son of Mary of Jerusalem: Acts 12:12
Not one of twelve apostles: Matt. 10:2–4

WRITTEN
To: Romans (Gentiles)
From: Rome (probably)

THE BOOK

Number in Bible	41
Number in N.T.	2
Chapters	16
Verses	678

PURPOSE

To present our Lord Jesus Christ as the Servant

DIVISIONS

Three Main Divisions of Mark

1. Introduction and identification of Servant
2. Miracles and ministry of Servant
3. From transfiguration to ascension

OUTLINE

I. The Servant Gives His Life in Service: Chapters 1–10.
    A. Servant's Work: chaps. 1–3
        1. Work begun: chap. 1
        2. Work belittled: chaps. 2:1–3:6
        3. Work blessed: chap. 3:7–19
        4. Work blasphemed: chap. 3:20–25
    B. Servant's Words: chaps. 4–5
        1. Exact in purpose: chap. 4:1–34
        2. Executive in power: chaps. 4:35–5:43
    C. Servant's Ways: chaps. 6:1–8:26
        1. Attitude of Others Toward God's Servant: chap. 6:1–29
        2. Actions for Others by God's Servant: chap. 6:30–8:26
    D. Servant's Worth: chaps. 8:27–9:13
    E. Servant's Will: chap. 9:14–29
    F. Servant's Wisdom: chaps. 9:30–10:52
II. The Servant Gives His Life in Sacrifice: Chapters 11–16.
    A. Previews the Crisis of Calvary: chaps. 11–12

B. Portrays the Consequences of Calvary: chap. 13:1–14:31

C. Permits the Cross of Calvary: chaps. 14:32–15:47

D. Proves the Crime of Calvary: chap. 16

    1. By conquering the grave: chap. 16:1–14

    2. By circling the globe: chap. 16:15–20

MISCELLANEOUS

Mark blessed with:

1. Godly home: Acts 12:12

2. Godly companions: Acts 12:25

3. Godly service: II Tim. 4:11

THE GOSPEL OF LUKE
The Son of Man

KEY VERSE: Luke 19:10

"For the Son of man is come to seek and to save that which was lost."

KEY WORDS
"Son of man"—used 26 times
1st use: chap. 5:24
Most significant use: chap. 19:10

THEME
The humanity of Christ (the perfect Man)

DATE
A.D. 60

WRITER
Luke
A Gentile
A Greek
Educated man
Keen observer
Not one of twelve apostles
Companion of Paul
Only non-Jewish writer of N. T.
Author of the Book of Acts
A medical doctor
Native of Syria

WRITTEN
To: Theophilus: *theos*=God; *phileo*=love—"lover of God"
From: Caesarea (likely)

THE BOOK
Number in Bible	42
Number in N.T.	3
Chapters	24
Verses	1,151

PURPOSE
1. To set in order the circumstances and events surrounding the life and ministry of our Lord
2. To give assurance and faith to those who follow Him

DIVISIONS
1. Introduction: chap. 1:1–4
2. Background: chaps. 1:5–2:52
3. Beginning of His Ministry: chaps. 3:1–4:13
4. Ministry in Galilee: chaps. 4:14–9:50
5. Journey to Jerusalem: chaps. 9:51–19:45
6. Last Week in Jerusalem: chaps. 19:45–23:56
7. Resurrection and Ascension: chap. 24

OUTLINE
Introduction (Prologue): chap. 1:1–4
I. Events Relating to the Saviour's Coming: Chapters 1:5–4:13
   A. His Birth at Bethlehem: chaps. 1:5–2:39
   B. His Boyhood at Nazareth: chap. 2:40–52
   C. His Baptism at Jordan: chap. 3:1–22
   D. His Background in History: chap. 3:23–38
   E. His Battle With Satan: chap. 4:1–13

II. Events Relating to the Saviour's Commission: Chapters 4:14–21:38
   A. The Work in Galilee: chaps. 4:14–9:50
      1. Work commenced: chaps. 4:14–5:17
      2. Work criticized: chaps. 5:18–6:11
      3. Work climaxed: chaps. 6:12–9:50
   B. The Way to Golgotha: chaps. 9:51–21:38
      His enemies used a variety of approaches to stop Him:
      1. Scholastic approach: chaps. 9:51–10:42
      2. Slanderous approach: chap. 11:1–28
      3. Sophisticated approach: chap. 11:29–52
      4. Systematic approach: chaps. 11:53–13:9
      5. Sermonic approach: chap. 13:10–30
      6. Scare approach: chap. 13:31–35
      7. Subtle approach: chap. 14
      8. Sarcastic approach: chap. 15
      9. Scoffing approach: chaps. 16:1–17:10
      10. Selfish approach: chap. 17:11–19
      11. Snobbish approach: chaps. 17:20–19:27
      12. Straightforward approach: chaps. 19:28–20:19
      13. Seductive approach: chaps. 20:20–21:38
III. Events Relating to the Saviour's Cross: Chapters 22–24
   A. Table: chap. 22:1–38
   B. Tears: chap. 22:39–53
   C. Trials: chaps. 22:54–23:31
   D. Tree: chap. 23:32–49
   E. Tomb: chap. 23:50–56
   F. Triumph: chap. 24

MISCELLANEOUS

Things mentioned only in Luke
1. The full particulars of the mystery of the virgin birth
2. Visit of the shepherds
3. Childhood of Jesus: visit to temple at age twelve
4. Emphasis on the Manhood of Jesus
    a. Toiled with hands
    b. Wept over city
    c. Suffered while kneeling in prayer
5. Healing Malchus' ear
6. Gospel to outcasts
    a. Good Samaritan: chap. 10:33
    b. Prodigal: chap. 15:11
    c. Publican: chap. 18:13
    d. Zacchaeus: chap. 19:2
7. Bloody sweat in Gethsemane: chap. 22:44

Facts about Luke
1. Devoted to God: Acts 21:14
2. Obsessed with compassion: Acts 16:10
3. Consecrated to work: II Tim. 4:11
4. Talented in his field: Col. 4:14
5. Observant of facts: Luke 1:4; Acts 1:1, 2
6. Reliable in tasks: Philem. 24
7. Loved by fellow workers: Col. 4:14; Acts 21:17
8. Understood the Gospel: Luke 1:3
9. Kind to all: Acts 21:1–11
10. Enjoyed the blessings of God: Acts 16:13–15; 28:10

THE GOSPEL OF JOHN
The Son of God

KEY VERSES: John 20:30, 31

"And many other signs truly did Jesus in the presence of his disciples, which are not written in this book:

"But these are written, that ye might believe that Jesus is the Christ, the Son of God; and that believing ye might have life through his name."

KEY WORD
"Believe"—used 52 times
1st use: chap. 1:7
Most significant use: chap. 20:31

THEME
The deity of Christ—"Son of God"

DATE
A.D. 90

WRITER
John the apostle
Youngest of twelve disciples
Brother of James
Son of Zebedee and Salome (believed to be Mary's sister)
Called 'son of thunder' when chosen by Jesus (diamond in the rough)
Grew up in Galilee
In fishing business: partners with James, Andrew and Peter
Disciple of John the Baptist
Closest to Jesus ("that disciple whom Jesus loved")

Wrote five books: John; I, II, III John; Revelation (fifty chapters)

WRITTEN
To: "whosoever"
From: Ephesus, before his exile to Patmos

THE BOOK
Number in Bible	43
Number in N.T.	4
Chapters	21
Verses	879

PURPOSE
To reveal Jesus as the Christ, the Messiah of Israel, that men might believe and be saved by trusting Christ as their personal Saviour

DIVISIONS
1. Ministry to Multitudes
   a. Coming of the Son of God: chaps. 1–4
   b. Claims by the Son of God: chaps. 5–7
   c. Confrontation With the Son of God: chaps. 8–10
   d. Coronation of the Son of God: chaps. 11–12
2. Ministry to Disciples
   a. Comfort by the Son of God: chaps. 13–17
   b. Crucifixion of the Son of God: chaps. 18–21

OUTLINE
Introduction: Chap. 1:1–18
I. Public Ministry of Christ: Chapters 1:19–12:50
   A. Confronting Individuals: chaps. 1:19–4:54
   B. Confronting Multitudes: chaps. 5:1–6:71

C. Conflicting With Multitudes: chaps. 7:1–11:53
D. Climax of Public Ministry: chaps. 11:54–12:50
II. Private Ministry of Christ: Chapters 13:1–17:26
    A. Last Supper: chap. 13:1–30
    B. Final Discourse: chaps. 13:31–16:33
    C. High Priestly Prayer: chap. 17:1–26
III. Passion Ministry of Christ: Chapters 18:1–20:31
    A. Betrayal and Trials: chaps. 18:1–19:16
    B. Crucifixion: chap. 19:17–42
    C. Resurrection: chap. 20
IV. Post-Resurrection Ministry of Christ: Chapter 21

MISCELLANEOUS

Seven famous miracles in John
1. Water to Wine (chap. 2): Power Over Quality
2. Nobleman's Son Healed (chap. 4): Power Over Distance
3. Infirmed Man Healed (chap. 5): Power Over Time
4. Feeding of the 5,000 (chap. 6): Power Over Quantity
5. Walking on Water (chap. 6): Power Over Nature
6. Blind Man Healed (chap. 9): Power Over Helplessness
7. Lazarus Raised (chap. 11): Power Over Death

Seven "I am's" in the Book of John
1. "I am the bread": chap. 6:35
2. "I am the light": chap. 8:12
3. "I am the door": chap. 10:9
4. "I am the good shepherd": chap. 10:11
5. "I am the resurrection": chap. 11:25
6. "I am the way, the truth, and the life": chap. 14:6
7. "I am the true vine": chap. 15:1

Digest of the New Testament ————————————————————

Title for each chapter in John

1. Beginning	12. Greek
2. Marriage	13. Passover
3. Nicodemus	14. Peace
4. Nobleman	15. Vine
5. Infirmed Man	16. Spirit
6. Bread	17. Prayer
7. Feast	18. Gethsemane
8. Light	19. Cross
9. Sight	20. Resurrection
10. Shepherd	21. Fishing
11. Lazarus	

ACTS
The Ascending Lord

KEY VERSE: Acts 1:8

"But ye shall receive power, after that the Holy Ghost is come upon you: and ye shall be witnesses unto me both in Jerusalem, and in all Judæa, and in Samaria, and unto the uttermost part of the earth."

KEY WORD
> "Witness" ("witnesses")—used 21 times
> > 1st use: chap. 1:8
> > Most significant use: chap. 1:8

THEME
> Power of God for witnessing

DATE
> A.D. 63 (covers a period of 32 years)

WRITER
> Luke (Acts 1:1; Luke 1:3; II Tim. 4:11)

WRITTEN
> To: Theophilus ("lover of God," "friend of God")
> From: Rome

THE BOOK

Number in Bible	44
Number in N.T.	5
Chapters	28
Verses	1,007

PURPOSE
To set forth God's plan for witnessing to the lost

In the key verse (chap. 1:8), the disciples were told to witness in Jerusalem, Judea, Samaria and the uttermost part of the earth.

DIVISIONS
1. The witness in Jerusalem recorded: chaps. 1–7
2. The witness in Judea and Samaria recorded: chaps. 8–12
3. The witness in the uttermost part of the earth recorded: chaps. 13–28

OUTLINE
I. Peter and the Church at Jerusalem: Chapters 1–12 (Jews)
   A. Church empowered in Upper Room: chaps. 1–2
   B. Church established in Jerusalem: chaps. 3–7
      1. Early persecution: chaps. 3–5
      2. First martyr: chaps. 6–7
   C. Church extended to Judea and Samaria: chaps. 8–9
   D. Church enlightened concerning Gentiles: chaps. 10–12
II. Paul and the Church at Antioch: Chapters 13–28 (Gentiles)
   A. Church enjoined to send missionaries: chap. 13:1–3
   B. Church enlarged to uttermost parts: chaps. 13:4–28:31
      1. First missionary trip: chaps. 13:4–14:28
      2. First church council: chap. 15:1–35
      3. Second missionary trip: chaps. 15:36–21:13
      4. Paul's arrest and imprisonment: chaps. 21:14–28:31

MISCELLANEOUS
Key men in Acts
   1. God's Man, Simon
   2. God's Martyr, Stephen
   3. God's Missionary, Saul

18

Acts gives particular attention to the following:
1. The Person: Lord Jesus Christ
2. The power: Holy Spirit
3. The preachers: Peter, Paul, Stephen, Philip
4. The places: Jerusalem, Antioch, Rome
5. The program: missions, witnessing

The Book of Acts
1. Covers a thirty-two-year span of time
2. Records the acts of the Holy Spirit
3. Contains numerous sermons on the death, burial and resurrection of Christ
4. Is a record of actual history
5. Is an instruction manual for Christians
6. Gives an exposition of Christian doctrines
7. Contains a number of thumbnail biographies
8. Has a strong missionary emphasis
9. Records several notable conversion stories
10. Stirs revival and builds up those who read it

Chapter Content
1. Ascension
2. Pentecost
3. Temple
4. Persecution
5. Ananias
6. Deacons
7. Stephen
8. Ethiopian
9. Conversion
10. Cornelius
11. Christians
12. Prayer
13. Missions
14. Iconium
15. Counsel
16. Philippi
17. Athens
18. Corinth
19. Ephesus
20. Elders
21. Arrest
22. Testimony
23. Sanhedrin
24. Felix
25. Festus
26. Agrippa
27. Shipwreck
28. Rome

Several Missionaries in Acts
1. Barnabas   Missionary Exhorter   chap. 11:22, 23
2. Saul   Missionary Teacher   chap. 11:25, 26
3. John Mark   Missionary Helper   chap. 13:5
4. Silas   Missionary Evangelist   chap. 15:40, 41
5. Timothy   Missionary Pastor   chap. 16:1
6. Luke   Missionary Doctor   chap. 16:10–13
7. Apollos   Missionary Orator   chap. 18:24, 27, 28
8. Aquila   Missionary Tentmaker   chap. 18:18
9. Priscilla   Missionary Assistant   chap. 18:2, 18, 26

Differences in Early Church and Present Church

Then	Now
Receptive to Word	Rebellious to Word
Obedient to Spirit	Disobedient to Spirit
Added to church	Subtracted from church
Continued in prayer	Ceased praying
Steadfast in service	Unstable in service
Fearful of God	No fear of God
Sold possessions	Keep possessions
One accord	Discord
House to house	Church to church
Glad	Sad
Praised God	Praises man

ROMANS
The Great Doctrinal Platform

KEY VERSES: Romans 1:16,17

> *"For I am not ashamed of the gospel of Christ: for it is the power of God unto salvation to every one that believeth; to the Jew first, and also to the Greek.*
>
> *"For therein is the righteousness of God revealed from faith to faith: as it is written, The just shall live by faith."*

KEY WORDS

"Law"—used 78 times

    1st use: chap. 2:12

    Most significant use: chap. 3:28

"Faith"—used 39 times

    1st use: chap. 1:5

    Most significant use: chap. 1:17

THEME

1. Righteousness of God through Jesus Christ
2. Justification by faith
3. The Gospel (Good News) of Christ—the power of God to believers

DATE

A.D. 58

WRITER

Apostle Paul

WRITTEN
To: A small group of Jewish believers in Rome, possibly saved at Pentecost

From: Corinth (on third missionary journey)

THE BOOK
Number in Bible	45
Number in N.T.	6
Chapters	16
Verses	433

PURPOSE
1. To set forth the cardinal doctrines of Christianity
2. To tell of Paul's coming visit to Rome

DIVISIONS
1. How the Gospel Relates to Sinners: chaps. 1–3
2. How the Gospel Relates to Saints: chaps. 4–8
3. How the Gospel Relates to Select (Jews): chaps. 9–11
4. How the Gospel Relates to Servant: chaps. 12–16

OUTLINE
Introduction: chap. 1:1–17.
I. All Men Are Under Condemnation: Chapters 1:18–3:20.
   A. Gentiles were guilty: chap. 1:20.
      1. Shunned the law of nature: chap. 1:20
      2. Shunned the law of conscience: chap. 2:14–16
   B. Jews were guilty: chap. 3:9.
      1. Had greater privileges than the Gentiles: chap. 3:2
      2. Had the oracles of God: chap. 3:2
II. Salvation Came Through Faith in Christ: Chapters 3:21–8:39.
   A. Included Justification: chaps. 3:21–5:11
      1. God declaring men righteous: chap. 3:25, 26

2. Came through Christ: chap. 3:24
B. Included sanctification: chaps. 5:12–8:13
1. God making men righteous: chap. 5:19
2. Came through the obedience of Christ: chap. 5:19
C. Included glorification: chap. 8:14–39
1. Made believers heirs with God: chap. 8:17
2. Provided for the redemption of all nature: chap. 8:21
III. Jews Refused God's Righteousness: Chapters 9–11.
A. They had great opportunities: chap. 9:14, 15.
B. God was working His will in them: chap. 9:16.
C. They deliberately rebelled against God: chap. 10:21.
D. Their failure brought in the Gentiles: chap. 11:11.
IV. Christians Were to Live Righteous Lives: Chapters 12–16.
A. Their bodies were to be dedicated to God: chap. 12:1, 2.
B. They were to be righteous to those within: chap. 12:10.
C. They were to be righteous to those without: chap. 12:18.
D. They were to be obedient to civil authorities: chap. 13:1.
E. They were to be considerate of all: chap. 14:19.
F. They were to shun false teachers: chap. 16:17.

MISCELLANEOUS
The House of Romans
1. Vestibule: chap. 1:1–17
2. Room of Sin: chaps. 1:18–3:31
3. Room of Justification: chaps. 4, 5
4. Room of Sanctification: chaps. 6, 7
5. Room of Glorification: chaps. 8–11
6. Room of Service: chaps. 12–16
The Book of Romans is:
1. Oracles of God   Not opinions of men
2. Meat of Word   Not milk of Word

3. Front page	Not footnotes
4. Forethought	Not afterthought
5. Church truth	Not kingdom truth
6. Message of grace	Not message of law
7. Lovely saints in Christ	Not lost sheep of Israel

Righteousness in Romans

1. Required	chaps. 1, 2
2. Revealed	chap. 3
3. Received	chaps. 4, 5
4. Rejected	chaps. 9, 10
5. Reproduced	chaps. 12–16

Note—There are more Old Testament quotations in Romans than in all of the other epistles combined (seventy).

I CORINTHIANS
Order in the Church

KEY VERSE: I Corinthians 10:31

"Whether therefore ye eat, or drink, or whatsoever ye do, do all to the glory of God."

KEY WORDS

"Divisions"—used 3 times
  1st use: chap. 1:10
  Most significant use: chap. 1:10
"Contentions"—used 1 time
  1st use: chap. 1:11
  Most significant use: chap. 1:11

THEME

Trouble in the church

DATE

A.D. 56

WRITER

Apostle Paul

Born at Tarsus	Wrote 100 N.T. chapters
Jew (Roman citizen)	Great preacher
Father was a Pharisee	Great missionary
Taught by Gamaliel	Great writer
Baptized by Ananias	Wrote 14 N. T. books
Four mission journeys	Wrote with simplicity
Wrote with sincerity	Beheaded in Rome

Digest of the New Testament ————————————————

WRITTEN
To: Saints at Corinth (Gentile Greek believers, babes in Christ)
From: Ephesus: chap. 16:7, 8

THE BOOK
Number in Bible	46
Number in N.T.	7
Chapters	16
Verses	437

PURPOSE
To reprove and correct serious problems existing among members of the church at Corinth

DIVISIONS
1. To the Church Collectively: chaps. 1–11
2. To the Church Individually: chaps. 12–16

1. Wisdom of Man vs. Revelation of God: chaps. 1–4
2. Worldliness of Man vs. Holiness of God: chaps. 5–9
3. Religion of Man vs. Holy Spirit of God: chaps. 10–16

OUTLINE
Disorders of the Church

I. Personal Disorders: Chapters 1–4
The problem: following men: chap. 1:12
The cure: exalting Christ: chap. 1:31

II. Moral Disorders: Chapters 5–6
The problem: yielding to the flesh: chap. 6:12
The cure: living in Christ: chap. 6:15

III. Home Disorders: Chapter 7:1
The problem: wrong ideas: chap. 7
The cure: benevolence and obedience: chap. 7:3

IV. Social Disorders: Chapters 8–10
  The problem: misused liberty: chap. 8:2
  The cure: the glory of God: chap. 10:31

V. Church Disorders: Chapters 11–14
  The problem: misconduct in worship: chap. 11:17, 18
  The cure: orderliness and temperance: chap. 14:32–40

VI. Doctrinal Disorders: Chapter 15
  The problem: denial of resurrection: chap. 15:12
  The cure: the risen Christ: chap. 15:20

VII. Financial Disorders: Chapter 16
  The problem: wrong motives: chap. 16:14
  The cure: tithes and offerings: chap. 16:2

MISCELLANEOUS

City of Corinth

1. Most important city of Greece (capital of Achaia, a Roman province)
2. Population of 500,000
3. Worshiped the goddess of love (Venus)
4. Corinth was on the trade route between East and West.
5. Was known for commerce, culture and corruption
6. Paul was in Corinth for one and one-half years (second missionary journey).
7. Paul met Aquila and Priscilla in Corinth (Acts 18).
8. Silas and Timothy joined to help Paul in Corinth (Acts 18).
9. Ruler of synagogue saved in Corinth (Crispus and Sosthenes—Acts 18)
10. People of Corinth were from a wicked background.
11. People of Corinth were a lower class of society.

I Corinthians	Written to new, immature believers
II Corinthians	Shows their progress and deals with comfort and maturity

False gods from the Garden to the Corinthians

Garden	Serpent
Romans	Bacchus
Phoenicians	Baal
Israelites	Golden calf
Ammonites	Moloch (fire god)
Athenians	Athena
Egyptians	Ra (sun god)
Corinthians	Venus (goddess of love)

The Church

The account of the founding of the church of Corinth is given in Acts 18:1–18. When Paul visited Corinth, it was the largest and most important city in Greece. In the midst of almost hopeless conditions, Paul preached "Christ crucified...the power of God, and the wisdom of God" (I Cor. 1:23, 24).

II CORINTHIANS
Help for the Afflicted

KEY VERSES: II Corinthians 1:3, 4

"Blessed be God, even the Father of our Lord Jesus Christ, the Father of mercies, and the God of all comfort;

"Who comforteth us in all our tribulation, that we may be able to comfort them which are in any trouble, by the comfort wherewith we ourselves are comforted of God."

KEY WORDS
"Comfort"—used 7 times
> 1st use: chap. 1:3
> Most significant use: chap. 1:3, 4

"Ministry"—used 3 times
> 1st use: chap. 4:1
> Most significant use: chap. 5:18

THEME
In trials and pressure, Christ is the believer's comfort.

DATE
A.D. 58

WRITER
Apostle Paul (see I Cor.)

WRITTEN
To: Believers at Corinth in Greece
From: Philippi

THE BOOK

Number in Bible	47
Number in N.T.	8
Chapters	13
Verses	257

PURPOSE

1. To strengthen the brethren in time of persecution
2. To restate Paul's apostolic authority
3. To magnify the Gospel of Christ
4. To challenge the Corinthians to faithful stewardship
5. To exalt the Person and work of Christ

DIVISIONS

1. Paul's Converts: chaps. 1–4
2. Paul's Conflicts: chaps. 5–7
3. Paul's Convictions: chaps. 8, 9
4. Paul's Consolation: chaps. 12, 13

OUTLINE

Paul's second epistle to the church at Corinth is difficult to present in outline form. He rushes from one theme to another, often repeating himself for the sake of emphasis.

Introduction: Chapter 1:1, 2

I. The Ministry of Suffering: Chapter 1:3–11
   A. Tribulation and consolation: chap. 1:3–7
   B. Paul's own suffering: chap. 1:8–11
II. Steadfastness of Paul's Purpose: Chapters 1:12–2:2
   A. His original plan: chap. 1:12–16
   B. His stability of mind: chap. 1:17–22
   C. The reason for his postponed visit: chaps. 1:23–2:2
III. Advice Concerning the Corinthian Offender: Chapter 2:3–11
   A. Reason for Paul's first epistle: chap. 2:3, 4

B. The necessity of forgiveness: chap. 2:5–11

IV. Paul's Personal Experiences: Chapters 2:12,13; 7:2–16
    A. His itinerary: chap. 2:12,13
    B. His anxiety: chaps. 2:13; 7:2–5
    C. His meeting with Titus: chap. 7:6
    D. His subsequent rejoicing: chap. 7:7, 13, 16

V. The Ministry of Reconciliation: Chapters 2:14–7:1
    A. Victorious: chap. 2:14–17
    B. Accredited: chap. 3:1–5
    C. Glorious: chap. 3:6–18
    D. Illuminating: chap. 4:1–6
    E. Costly: chaps. 4:7–5:8
    F. Motivated: chap. 5:9–21
    G. Demanding: chap. 6:1–10
    H. Divisive: chaps. 6:11–7:1

VI. The Summons to Stewardship: Chapters 8:1–9:15
    A. Macedonian example: chap. 8:1–6
    B. Appeal to generosity: chap. 8:7–15
    C. Mission of Titus: chaps. 8:16–9:5
    D. Challenge to liberality: chap. 9:6–14
    E. Gratitude for Christ—the supreme Gift: chap. 9:15

VII. Vindication of Paul's Ministry: Chapters 10:1–12:13
    A. Accusations against him: chaps. 10:1–10; 13:3
    B. Object of his glorying: chap. 10:11–18
    C. Corinthians' gullibility: chap. 11:1–4
    D. Paul's proven apostolic authority: chaps. 11:5–12:13

VIII. Paul's Proposed Journey: Chapters 12:14–13:10
    A. Its purpose: chap. 12:14–18
    B. An advance warning: chaps. 12:19–13:10

Conclusion: Chapter 13:11–14

MISCELLANEOUS
Chapter Content:
Afflictions and comfort: chap. 1
Approaching the fallen: chap. 2
Approving the counselor: chap. 3
Accepting our ministry: chap. 4
Attitude toward death: chap. 5
Asking for endurance and separation: chap. 6
Admonition to cleansing: chap. 7
Advice on giving: chap. 8
Abounding in reaping: chap. 9
Awareness in need: chap. 10
Assurance of Paul's calling: chap. 11
Account of the revelation to Paul: chap. 12
Appeal to hear God: chap. 13

Christian's Sevenfold Duty
1. Love the fallen: chap. 2:5–13
2. Testify to the unsaved: chap. 2:14–17
3. Live consistently: chaps. 3–6
4. Receive correction: chap. 7
5. Give cheerfully: chaps. 8, 9
6. Acknowledge authority: chap. 10:1–8
7. Prove ourselves: chap. 13:5–14

GALATIANS
The Magna Carta of Christian Freedom

KEY VERSE: Galatians 5:1

"Stand fast therefore in the liberty wherewith Christ hath made us free, and be not entangled again with the yoke of bondage."

KEY WORDS
"Law"—used 32 times
1st use: chap. 2:16
Most significant use: chap. 2:16
"Faith"—used 22 times
1st use: chap. 1:23
Most significant use: chap. 3:11
"Free"—used 4 times
1st use: chap. 3:28
Most significant use: chap. 5:1

THEME
Liberty, not bondage
God has given liberty to believers in Christ. We are not to be entangled again with the yoke of bondage (the law).

DATE
A.D. 55

WRITER
Apostle Paul

WRITTEN
To: Believers in Galatia
From: Rome

THE BOOK

Number in Bible	48
Number in N.T.	9
Chapters	6
Verses	149

PURPOSE

To refute and offset the teachings of the Judaizers, who were teaching that after salvation was obtained through Christ, it must be maintained by works

DIVISIONS

1. The Cross and Deliverance From an Evil World: chap. 1
2. The Cross and Crucifixion: chap. 2
3. The Cross and Redemption From Curse: chap. 3
4. The Cross and Adoption Into Sonship: chap. 4
5. The Cross and Its Continued Offense: chap. 5
6. The Cross and Its Persecutions: chap. 6

OUTLINE

I. Personal: Grace and the Gospel: Chapters 1, 2
    A. Grace declared in Paul's message: chap. 1:1–10
    B. Grace demonstrated in Paul's life: chap. 1:11–24
    C. Grace defended in Paul's ministry: chap. 2:1–21
        1. Before the church leaders collectively: chap. 2:1–10
        2. Before Peter personally: chap. 2:11–21
II. Doctrinal: Grace and the Law: Chapters 3, 4
    Paul proves salvation is not through keeping the law.
    A. Personal argument from experience: chap. 3:1–5
    B. Scriptural argument—Abraham's faith: chap. 3:6–14
    C. Logical argument: chap. 3:15–29
    D. Dispensational argument: chap. 4:1–11

E. Sentimental argument: chap. 4:12–18

F. Allegorical argument: chap. 4:19–31

III. Practical: Grace and the Christian Life: Chapters 5, 6

A. Liberty—not bondage: chap. 5:1–5

B. The Spirit—not the flesh: chap. 5:16–26

C. Others—not self: chap. 6:1–10

D. God's glory—not man's approval: chap. 6:11–18

MISCELLANEOUS

1. Galatians is called "Paul's explosive epistle"—every sentence is a thunderbolt; every word is a stick of dynamite.

2. Relates to the Book of Romans

In Galatians we find:

1. A *law* that had been satisfied

2. A *love* that had been manifested

3. A *life* that must be lived

4. A *liberty* that had been secured

EPHESIANS
The Heavenlies

KEY VERSES: Ephesians 2:8, 9

"For by grace are ye saved through faith; and that not of yourselves: it is the gift of God:
"Not of works, lest any man should boast."

KEY WORDS

"Grace"—used 12 times
1st use: chap. 1:2
Most significant use: chap. 2:8
"Body"—used 9 times
1st use: chap. 1:23
Most significant use: chap. 1:23
"Walk"—used 7 times
1st use: chap. 2:10
Most significant use: chap. 2:10

THEME

As a part of the body of Christ, the believer has been given a heavenly position and should conduct himself in light of that position.

DATE

A.D. 64

WRITER

Apostle Paul (see I Cor.)

WRITTEN

To: Believers (saints) at Ephesus
From: Rome (one of four prison epistles: Ephesians,

Philippians, Philemon, Colossians)

THE BOOK

Number in Bible	49
Number in N.T.	10
Chapters	6
Verses	155

PURPOSE

1. To strengthen believers in their faith
2. To encourage them to walk worthy of their position
3. To reveal the mystery that all believers (Jews and Gentiles) are members of the body of Christ

DIVISIONS

1. Going Into the Mountains to Worship: chaps. 1–3
2. Going Into the Meadows to Walk: chaps. 4–6

1. Creed—Doctrine: What We Believe: chaps. 1–3
2. Conduct—Deportment: How We Behave: chaps. 4–6

OUTLINE

The Church in Christ

I. Its Origin: Chapter 1
  A. Selected by the Father: vs. 4
  B. Saved by the Son: vs. 7
  C. Sealed by the Spirit: vs. 13

II. Its Formation: Chapter 2
  A. Raised: vs. 5
  B. Re-created: vs. 10
  C. Reconciled: vs. 16
  D. Reunited: vs. 19

III. Its Design: Chapter 3

A. The plan: vss. 1–6
B. The power: vss. 7–12
C. The purpose: vss. 13–20
D. The praise: vs. 21
IV. Its Duties: Chapters 4–6
  A. To Walk
    1. In unity: chap. 4:1–16
    2. In purity: chap. 4:17–32
    3. In love: chap. 5:1–6
    4. In light: chap. 5:7–14
    5. In caution: chap. 5:15–17
    6. In harmony: chaps. 5:18–6:9
  B. To War
    1. The enemy with which we are fighting: chap. 6:10–12
    2. The equipment with which we are fitted: chap. 6:13–17
    3. The energy with which we are filled: chap. 6:18–24

MISCELLANEOUS

1. Blessings: chap. 1
2. Body: chap. 2
3. Building: chap. 3
4. Behavior: chap. 4
5. Bride: chap. 5
6. Battle: chap. 6

PHILIPPIANS
Book of Joy

KEY VERSE: Philippians 4:4

"Rejoice in the Lord alway: and again I say, Rejoice."

KEY WORD

"Joy" is used 6 times in 4 chapters. Someone has said that Paul's chains sound like "joy bells."

> 1st use: chap. 1:4
> Most significant use: chap. 4:1

THEME

1. God is all-sufficient to be the strength of the believer and to meet his needs.
2. Rejoice in the Lord regardless of the circumstances.

DATE

A.D. 63 (approximately); ten years after Paul was in Philippi

WRITER

Apostle Paul

WRITTEN

To: Believers at Philippi
From: Mamertine Prison in Rome

THE BOOK

Number in Bible	50
Number in N.T.	11
Chapters	4
Verses	104

PURPOSE

The Philippians had sent a gift to Paul by the hand of Epaphroditus (4:18) when he was in prison in Rome. While in Rome, Epaphroditus became seriously ill and on the verge of death (2:27). The Philippians were concerned over his illness, and Epaphroditus was disturbed by their concern and longed to see them (2:26). After he recovered, Paul sent him back to the Philippians (2:25) for the following reasons:

1. To thank them for their gift
2. To express his love for them
3. To tell of his work and release
4. To warn them of dangers

DIVISIONS

1. The Believer Rejoices in Suffering: chap. 1.
2. The Believer Rejoices in Service: chap. 2.
3. The Believer Rejoices in Spite of Imperfections: chap. 3.
4. The Believer Rejoices Over Anxiety: chap. 4.

OUTLINE

I. The Inward Look—the Testimony of a Christian: Chapter 1
  A. Christ is our passion.
  B. We live for him.

II. The Backward Look—the Temperament of a Christian: Chapter 2
  A. Christ is our pattern.
  B. We labor for Him.

III. The Forward Look—the Treasury of a Christian: Chapter 3
  A. Christ is our prize.
  B. We look to Him.

IV. The Upward Look—the Triumph of a Christian:
Chapter 4
  A. Christ is our power.
  B. We learn of Him.

MISCELLANEOUS

1. Christ is mentioned 38 times in Philippians.
2. Sin is not the focus of the book.
3. Philippians is one of four prison epistles: Philippians, Ephesians, Colossians, Philemon.
4. Addressed to three groups: saints, bishops and deacons
5. Background in Acts 16
6. Delivered by Epaphroditus
7. The church was established on Paul's second missionary journey.
8. The church began with three converts: Lydia, a demon-possessed girl and the Philippian jailer.

Christ in Philippians
    We are to:
    Preach Christ   chap. 1:15, 16
    Live Christ   chap. 1:20, 21
    Confess Christ   chap. 2:10
    Trust Christ   chap. 2:19–24
    Win Christ   chap. 3:8
    Know Christ   chap. 3:10
    Expect Christ   chap. 3:20

Happy Mind   Christ Our Life—chap. 1
Humble Mind   Christ Our Mind—chap. 2
Heavenly Mind   Christ Our Goal—chap. 3
Holy Mind   Christ Our Power—chap. 4

COLOSSIANS
The Preeminence of Christ

KEY VERSE: Colossians 1:18

"...that in all things he might have the preeminence."

KEY WORDS

"Head"—used 3 times
1st use: chap. 1:18
Most significant use: chap. 1:18
"Fulness"—used 2 times
1st use: chap. 1:19
Most significant use: chap. 2:9

THEME

God's fullness in Jesus
1. He is Head of the church (which is His body).
2. He is Creator of the universe.

DATE

A.D. 62

WRITER

Apostle Paul

WRITTEN

To: Church at Colossae (mostly Gentile converts)
From: Mamertine Prison in Rome; delivered by Tychicus and Onesimus (chap. 4:7–9)

THE BOOK

Number in Bible	51
Number in N.T.	12
Chapters	4
Verses	95

PURPOSE

Paul wrote that these believers might be aware of their

Inheritance in Christ	chap. 1:12
Deliverance through Christ	chap. 1:13
Translation in Christ	chap. 1:13
Redemption in Christ	chap. 1:14
Forgiveness by Christ	chap. 1:14
Reconciliation by Christ	chap. 1:21
Presentation by Christ	chap. 1:22

DIVISIONS

1. Doctrinal: To show how to be filled with the Spirit: chap. 1, 2
2. Practical: To help us be faithful in service: chap. 3,4

OUTLINE

Introduction

Paul identified the Person of Christ as the Creator, the divine Head of the universe. He discusses the believers completeness in Him.

As a result of what Christ has done for the believer, the Christian is encouraged to conduct himself accordingly by 'putting off the old man' and 'putting on the new man.'

CHRIST IS SUPREME

I. Through Prayer: Chap. 1:1–12

II. In Creation and Redemption: Chap. 1:13–18

III. In Reconciliation: Chap. 1:19–23

IV. In Christian Faith: Chap. 2:4–7

V. In Doctrine: Chap. 2:8–15
VI. In Religion: Chap. 2:6–23
VII. In Spiritual Life: Chap. 3:1–11
VIII. In Risen Life: Chap. 3:12–17
IX. In Human Relationships: Chap. 3:18–4:1
X. In Christian Service: Chap. 4:2–9
XI. In Friendship: Chap. 4:10–18

MISCELLANEOUS

1. Church at Colossae was probably founded by Epaphras (chap. 4:12).
2. Paul likely had not visited this church.
3. Paul had many friends among its members.
4. Onesimus had come from there (chap. 4:9).
5. Archippus was probably Philemon's son (Philem. 2).
6. Archippus was possibly pastor there (chap. 4:17).
7. Epaphras was likely in prison with Paul (Philem. 23).
8. There is a similarity between Ephesians and Colossians.

I THESSALONIANS
Watch

KEY VERSE: I Thessalonians 4:16

"For the Lord himself shall descend from heaven with a shout, with the voice of the archangel, and with the trump of God: and the dead in Christ shall rise first."

KEY WORDS

"Coming"—used 4 times
> 1st use: chap. 2:19
> Most significant use: chap. 4:15

"Comfort"—used 4 times
> 1st use: chap. 3:2
> Most significant use: chap. 4:18

Jesus is referred to as "Lord" 25 times in I Thessalonians.

THEME

Christ's return: the believer's Hope

DATE

A.D. 53

Paul was approximately 46 years old and had been saved for 16 years.

WRITER

Apostle Paul

WRITTEN

To: The saints at Thessalonica (mostly Gentiles)
From: Corinth, on second missionary journey

THE BOOK

Number in Bible	52
Number in N.T.	13
Chapters	5
Verses	89

PURPOSE

1. To strengthen and confirm new Christians
2. To answer false accusations about Paul
3. To explain that the Christian dead would participate in the rapture
4. To warn Christians about pagan immorality
5. To remind Christian members to honor and follow scriptural leaders
6. To warn members not to give up jobs and wait

DIVISIONS

1. Recognition of how they were saved, dealt with and cared for
2. Reminder of how to live to please God

OUTLINE

I. People in the Church: Chapter 1
   A. Elect: vs. 4
   B. Example: vs. 7
   C. Enthusiastic: vs. 8
   D. Expectant: vs. 10

II. Preacher in the Church: Chapter 2
   A. Faithful Steward: vs. 4
   B. Gentle Mother: vs. 7
   C. Concerned Father: vs. 11
   D. Loving Brother: vs. 14

III. Program in the Church: Chapter 3
   A. Involved a Man Sent From God: vs. 2

B. Involved a Letter Written by Paul: vs. 2

C. Involved a Prayer by Paul: vs. 10

D. Involved a Reminder of the Second Coming: vs. 13

IV. Plan for the Church: Chapter 4

    A. Walk in Holiness: vs. 7

    B. Walk in Love: vs. 9

    C. Walk in Honesty: vs. 12

    D. Walk in Hope: vs. 13

V. Prospect for the Church: Chapter 5

    A. Walk in Light: vss. 1–11

    B. Walk in Gratitude: vss. 12, 13

    C. Walk in Obedience: vss. 14–28

MISCELLANEOUS

Chronological order of Paul's books

1. Prophetic—I and II Thessalonians
2. Platform (doctrinal)—Romans, I and II Corinthians, Galatians
3. Prison Epistles—Colossians, Ephesians, Philippians, Philemon
4. Pastoral Epistles—I and II Timothy, Titus

Purpose of a church as seen in I Thessalonians

1. A center for getting out the Gospel: chap. 1:8
2. A nursery for new babes: chap. 2:7, 8
3. A target for the Devil: chaps. 2:14–3:5
4. A family circle abounding in love: chap. 3:12
5. A workshop of divine discipline: chap. 4:1, 3, 7
6. A school for character development: chap. 4:9–13
7. A hospital for the spiritually weak: chap. 5:14

Each chapter refers to the second coming.
>   His Coming and Salvation: chap. 1:10
>   His Coming and Service: chap. 2:9, 10
>   His Coming and Stability: chap. 3:13
>   His Coming and Sorrow: chap. 4:18
>   His Coming and Sanctification: chap. 5:23

II THESSALONIANS
The Day of the Lord

KEY VERSE: II Thessalonians 2:3

"Let no man deceive you by any means: for that day shall not come, except there come a falling away first, and that man of sin be revealed, the son of perdition."

KEY WORDS

"Come," "coming"—used 6 times
    1st use: chap. 1:10
    Most significant use: chap. 2:8
"Revealed"—used 4 times
    1st use: chap. 1:7
    Most significant use: chap. 2:3

THEME

Christians are to be patient in waiting, watching and working up to the Lord's return.

DATE

A.D. 53 (spring—three months after I Thessalonians was written)

WRITER

Apostle Paul

WRITTEN

To: Believers at Thessalonica
From: Corinth

THE BOOK

Number in Bible	53
Number in N.T.	14
Chapters	3
Verses	47

PURPOSE

1. To correct wrong views concerning the second coming
2. To comfort and encourage the faithful
3. To admonish the lazy and disorderly
4. To show believers how to conduct themselves while waiting on the Lord

DIVISIONS

1. The Second Coming and Comfort in Persecution: chap. 1
2. The Second Coming and the Coming Man of Sin: chap. 2
3. The Second Coming and Christians' Daily Living: chap. 3

OUTLINE

I. Encouragement in Suffering: Chapter 1
   A. Greeting and grace in time of persecution: vss. 1, 2
   B. Gratitude and growth in persecution: vss. 3–5
   C. Glorious and grand appearing of Christ to end persecution: vss. 6–10
   D. Goodness and glory because of persecution: vss. 11, 12
II. Enlightenment About the Day of the Lord: Chapter 2
   A. There will be a falling away: vss. 1–3.
   B. The Man of Sin will be revealed: vss. 3–5.
   C. The temple will be rebuilt: vs. 4.
   D. The Holy Spirit will be taken out of the way: vss. 6, 7.
   E. The world will be deceived: vss. 8–10.
   F. The church will be completed: vss. 13–17.

III. Establishment in Christian Living: Chapter 3
  A. Plea for Prayer and Patience: vss. 1–5
    1. Prayer: vs. 1
    2. Persecution: vs. 2
    3. Protection: vs. 3
    4. Practicing: vs. 4
    5. Patience: vs. 5
  B. Proclaiming the Problem: vss. 6–13
    1. Walking disorderly: vss. 6–11
    2. Workers idle: vss. 10,11
    3. Weary in welldoing: vs. 13
  C. Providing the Plan: vs. 12
    1. Work quietly and steadily: vs. 12
    2. Win own bread (self-sustaining): vs. 12
    3. Withdraw from worthless: vss. 6, 14
  D. Presenting the Program of Peace: vss. 14–18
    1. Watch disobedience: vs. 14
    2. Withdraw from disobedient: vs. 14
    3. Work with disobedient: vs. 15
    4. Wait for peace: vs. 16

MISCELLANEOUS

1. Along with Rome, it is the only city to which Paul wrote that has remained significant.
2. It is Greece's second largest city, with a metropolitan population over 800,000.
3. The founding of the church is recorded in Acts 17.
4. The Jews there were less noble than those in Berea.

I TIMOTHY
Instructing a Young Preacher

KEY VERSES: I Timothy 3:15, 16

"But if I tarry long, that thou mayest know how thou oughtest to behave thyself in the house of God, which is the church of the living God, the pillar and ground of the truth.

"And without controversy great is the mystery of godliness: God was manifest in the flesh, justified in the Spirit, seen of angels, preached unto the Gentiles, believed on in the world, received up into glory."

KEY WORDS
"Doctrine"—used 8 times
  1st use: chap. 1:3
  Most significant use: chap. 4:16
"Good"—used 23 times
  1st use: chap. 1:5
  Most significant use: chap. 6:12

THEME
The conduct of pastors and members
Qualifications of leaders

DATE
A.D. 63–64

WRITER
Apostle Paul

WRITTEN
To: Timothy (young pastor at Ephesus)

From: Rome (between two imprisonments)

THE BOOK
Number in Bible   54
Number in N.T.   15
Chapters   6
Verses   113

PURPOSE
Paul exhorts Timothy in Chapter 1 to
1. Stand firm: vs. 3
2. Speak up: vs. 4
3. Take care: vs. 18
4. Fight on: vs. 19
5. Keep true: vs. 20

DIVISIONS
1. How to Deal With Heresy: chap. 1
2. How to Regulate Church Life: chaps. 2, 3
3. How to Conduct Our Daily Living: chaps. 4–6

OUTLINE
I. Pure Doctrine: Chapter 1
  A. Paul's message was authentic: vs. 15.
  B. Paul's message was acceptable: vs. 15.
  C. Paul's message was adaptable: vs. 15.
II. Public Responsibility of Church: Chapter 2
  A. Public praying: vss. 1–8
  B. Presentable women: vss. 9–15
III. Prerequisites for Church Officers: Chapter 3
  A. Qualifications of pastors: vss. 1–7
  B. Qualifications of deacons: vss. 8–15
  C. Quality of their message: vs. 16

IV. Pastoral Pattern of Church: Chapter 4
  A. Expressed concern over false teachers: vss. 1–7
  B. Exhortation to young pastors: vss. 8–16
V. Preparation for Church Widows: Chapter 5
  A. Advice on relationships: vss. 1, 2
  B. Action toward widows: vss. 3–16
  C. Accountability of pastors: vss. 17–25
VI. Practical Conduct of Believers: Chapter 6
  A. Concerning servants: vss. 1, 2
  B. Concerning subversives: vss. 3–6
  C. Concerning substance: vss. 7–10
  D. Concerning soundness: vss. 11–21

MISCELLANEOUS

1. Timothy was the son of a Greek father and Jewish mother. (Acts 16:1)
2. He traveled widely with Paul and often served as his messenger.
3. He seems to have been timid at first (II Tim. 1:7), but tradition says he died a martyr for standing against an idolatrous celebration.

1. Gives his name as Paul (Latin—*Paulus*), (Saul—Hebrew name)
2. States his office: apostle, author, authority
3. Gives titles of the Lord: "Jesus," the Saviour; "Christ," the Sanctified; "Lord," the Sovereign

II TIMOTHY
The Good Fight

KEY VERSE: II Timothy 2:15

"Study to shew thyself approved unto God, a workman that needeth not to be ashamed, rightly dividing the word of truth."

KEY WORDS
"Suffer"—used 4 times
1st use: chap. 1:12
Most significant use: chap. 3:12
"Endure"—used 4 times
1st use: chap. 2:3
Most significant use: chap. 2:3

THEME
A challenge to endure pressures and affliction, to be strong in the face of apostasy

DATE
A.D. 67 (approximately)

WRITER
Apostle Paul

WRITTEN
To: Timothy at Ephesus
From: Prison in Rome

THE BOOK
Number in Bible   55
Number in N.T.   16

Chapters   4
Verses   83

PURPOSE
To encourage Timothy
1. To be bold and fearless
2. To be faithful in testings
3. To beware of apostasy in the future
4. To come to see him and to bring him needed possessions

DIVISIONS
1. Pastoral Appeal: Reminder of responsibility and privileges: chap. 1
2. Practical Appeal: Effort to solve some problems: chap. 2
3. Prophetic Appeal: Points out importance of holding fast: chap. 3
4. Personal Appeal: Appeal to Timothy to remain true: chap. 4

OUTLINE
I. Paul's Concern for Timothy: Chapter 1
   A. Remembering: vss. 1–6
   B. Resources: vss. 7–11
   C. Reward: vss. 12–18
II. Paul's Challenge to Timothy: Chapter 2
   A. Distribute the Word: vs. 2
   B. Dedication to battle: vss. 3,4
   C. Discipline in work: vs. 5
   D. Doing the work: vs. 6
   E. Diligence: vss. 7–10
   F. Dividing the Word: vs. 15
   G. Direction: vss. 22–26

III. Paul's Caution to Timothy: Chapter 3
    A. Perils of the last days: vs. 1
    B. People of the last days: vss. 2–5
    C. Plea to the true believer: vs. 5
    D. Program for the last days: vss. 10, 11
    E. Plan for the last days: vss. 14, 15
    F. Profit available in the last days: vss. 15–17
IV. Paul's Charge to Timothy: Chapter 4
    A. Preach the Word: vss. 1–4
    B. Prove your calling: vs. 5
    C. Personally illustrate your ministry: vss. 6–8
    D. Profit from experience and fellowship of others: vss. 10–22

MISCELLANEOUS
The Spread of Apostasy

I Timothy
    Some have turned aside: chap. 1:6.
    Some have made shipwreck: chap. 1:19.
    Some have turned aside after Satan: chap. 5:15.
    Some have been led astray: chap. 6:10.
    Some have erred: chap. 6:21.

II Timothy
    All have turned away from Paul: chap. 1:15.
    All forsook Paul: chap. 4:16.

TITUS
Instructing a Young Church

KEY VERSES: Titus 2:14; 3:8

"Who gave himself for us, that he might redeem us from all iniquity, and purify unto himself a peculiar people, zealous of good works."

"This is a faithful saying, and these things I will that thou affirm constantly, that they which have believed in God might be careful to maintain good works. These things are good and profitable unto men."

KEY WORDS
"Good works"—used 4 times
1st use: chap. 1:16
Most significant use: chap. 3:8

THEME
Blending sound faith and good works

DATE
A.D. 66–67, between first and second imprisonments, between I and II Timothy

WRITER
Apostle Paul
Artemas or Tychicus carried the pastoral letter for Paul.

WRITTEN
To: Titus
From: Rome (end of third missionary journey; one of Paul's last letters)

THE BOOK

Number in Bible	56
Number in N.T.	17
Chapters	3
Verses	46

PURPOSE

Paul left Titus on Crete in the Mediterranean Sea to complete his work of establishing and organizing churches into self-governing, self-supporting bodies.

This letter is to instruct Titus concerning qualifications for elders in the church, to warn against false teachers and to fortify Titus in his work.

DIVISIONS

1. Good Works in the House of God: chap. 1
2. Good Works in the Home of Men: chap. 2
3. Good Works in the Heathen World: chap. 3

OUTLINE

I. In the House of God: Chapter 1

  A. The fivefold description: vss. 1–4

    1. Paul describes himself: servant, apostle: vs. 1.

    2. Paul describes Christians: elect, believers: vs. 1.

    3. Paul describes the Gospel: eternal, declared: vs. 2.

    4. Paul describes the Lord: cannot lie: vs. 2.

    5. Paul describes Titus: Paul's own child: vs. 4.

  B. The faithful leaders: vss. 5–9

    1. Elders: experienced, mature: vs. 7

    2. Bishops: overseers: vs. 7

    3. Stewards: act on behalf of another: vs. 7

  C. The fakers and foolish in the church: vss. 10–15

    1. Were numerous: vs. 10

    2. Were disobedient: vs. 10

    3. Their teaching and actions affected by disobedience: vs. 11

    4. Were a bad influence: vs. 11

    5. Had impure natures: vs. 11

    6. Had bad background and temperament: vs. 12

    7. Were to be rebuked and stopped: vs. 13

II. In the Home of Men: Chapter 2

  A. Aged men will behave properly: vs. 2.

  B. Aged women will behave properly: vs. 3.

  C. Young women will behave properly: vss. 4, 5.

  D. Young men will behave properly: vs. 6.

  E. Servants will behave properly: vs. 9.

  F. Christians will behave properly: vss. 12, 13.

III. In the Heathen World: Chapter 3

  A. The Christian to respect authority: vss. 1–3

  B. The Christian to rejoice in assurance: vss. 4–8

  C. The Christian to reject the adversary: vss. 9–11

  D. The Christian to respond to appeal: vss. 12–15

MISCELLANEOUS

1. Titus was a Gentile convert of Paul's early ministry (Titus 1:4; Gal. 2:1–3).

2. He was another companion and messenger in Paul's travels, especially to Corinth (II Cor. 7, 8).

PHILEMON

Imputed Righteousness

KEY VERSE: Philemon 18

"If he hath wronged thee, or oweth thee ought, put that on mine account."

KEY WORD

"Profitable" is used 1 time. *Onesimus* means "profitable."
1st use: vs. 11
Most significant use: vs. 11

THEME

Paul intercedes with Philemon for Onesimus, a runaway slave.

DATE

A.D. 62

WRITER

Apostle Paul (vss. 1,19)

WRITTEN

To: Philemon, a wealthy Greek Christian landowner and slaveholder at Colossae (Philem. 1, 2, 10; Col. 4:9)

From: Rome, during Paul's first imprisonment there (house arrest: Acts 28:16, 30)

THE BOOK

Number in Bible   57
Number in N.T.   18

Chapters	1
Verses	25

PURPOSE

Onesimus, a slave of Philemon, probably stole from his master and ran away. In his travels, he met Paul in Rome, who converted him to Christ. Paul then sent him back to Philemon with Tychicus carrying this letter in which he was pleading and interceding for Onesimus.

DIVISIONS

1. Runaway Slave (Like Adam or Prodigal)
2. Regenerated Son
3. Reliable Servant
4. Respected Brother

OUTLINE

I. Paul Presents His Greeting: "Grace...and peace" (Shalom): Vss. 1–3

II. Paul Praised Philemon: 'Thank God for you': Vss. 4–8

III. Paul Pleads for Onesimus: "I beseech thee": Vss. 9–17

IV. Paul Pledges to Pay: "I will repay it": Vss. 18–22

V. Paul's Personal Request: "salute": Vss. 23–25

MISCELLANEOUS

Facts About Philemon
1. Wealthy land owner: vs. 16
2. Leading member of church at Colossae: vss. 4–7
3. Won to Christ by Paul: vs. 19
4. The church met in his house: vs. 2.
5. Owned slaves: vs. 16
6. His wife was possibly Apphia: vs. 2.

7. Archippus, possibly his son, may have been the pastor: Col. 4:17.

Uniqueness of the Epistle among Paul's writings
1. Short: 1 chapter, 25 verses
2. Personal
3. Revealing
   a. Paul's concern for individuals as well as groups
   b. Interest in spiritual condition of slaves as well as masters
   c. Determination to follow up after winning souls
4. Prison Epistle: private letter

HEBREWS
Superiority of Christ

KEY VERSE: Hebrews 4:14

"Seeing then that we have a great high priest, that is passed into the heavens, Jesus the Son of God, let us hold fast our profession."

KEY WORDS
"Better"—used 13 times
1st use: chap. 1:4
Most significant use: chap. 8:6
"Perfect"—used 9 times
1st use: chap. 2:10
Most significant use: chap. 7:19
"Heaven"—used 5 times
1st use: chap. 9:24
Most significant use: chap. 9:24

THEME
The priesthood of Christ
The maturity of believers

DATE
Between A.D. 64 and A.D. 67

WRITER
Apostle Paul

WRITTEN
To: A group of Jewish Christians
From: Italy (chap. 13:24)

THE BOOK

Number in Bible	58
Number in N.T.	19
Chapters	13
Verses	303

PURPOSE

1. To encourage persecuted Christians
2. To check apostasy
3. To show relationship between Jewish ordinances, covenants and Christianity

DIVISIONS

Twofold Division

Chapters 1–10	Chapters 11–13
Doctrine	Deportment
Belief	Behavior
Principle	Practice
Creed	Conduct

OUTLINE

I. A Superior Person: Christ: Chapters 1–6

    A. Greater than prophets: chap. 1:1–3

    B. Greater than angels: chaps. 1:4–2:18

    C. Greater than Moses: chap. 3:1–19

    D. Greater than Joshua: chap. 4:1–16

    E. Greater than Aaron: chaps. 5:1; 10:18

    F. Greater than Melchisedec: chap. 7:1, 15

II. A Superior Priesthood: Melchisedec: Chapters 7–10

    A. Better order: Melchisedec, not Aaron: chap. 7

    B. Better covenant: new, not old: chap. 8

    C. Better sanctuary: Heaven, not Earth: chap. 9

    D. Better Sacrifice: God's Son, not animals: chap. 10

III. A Superior Principle: Faith: Chapters 11–13

    A. Example of faith: chap. 11

    B. Endurance of faith: chap. 12

    C. Evidence of faith: chap. 13

MISCELLANEOUS

Warnings of Spiritual Deterioration: chap. 2:1–4

1. Drifting from the Word through neglect: chap. 2:3
2. Doubting the Word through hardness of heart: chap. 3:19
3. Dullness toward the Word through sluggishness: chap. 5:11
4. Despising the Word through willful sinning: chap. 10:26
5. Disobeying the Word by refusing to hear: chap. 12:25

Facts About Hebrews

1. Hebrews is referred to as "the fifth Gospel."
2. The first four Gospels deal with earthly ministry; this "fifth Gospel" deals with heavenly ministry.
3. There are 17 provoking questions in Hebrews.
4. There are 270 verses of history, 9 verses of fulfilled prophecy and 24 verses of unfulfilled prophecy.
5. Hebrews parallels the Old Testament's Book of Leviticus.

JAMES
Demonstrating Faith

KEY VERSE: James 1:5

"If any of you lack wisdom, let him ask of God, that giveth to all men liberally, and upbraideth not; and it shall be given him."

KEY WORDS

"Faith"—used 16 times
   1st use: chap. 1:3
   Most significant use: chap. 2:22
"Works"—used 13 times
   1st use: chap. 2:14
   Most significant use: chap. 2:18

THEME

Maturity:
1. Through persecution from without
2. Through problems from within

DATE

A.D. 45–50 (before the fall of Jerusalem)

WRITER

James

WRITTEN

To: Twelve tribes scattered in dispersion (chap. 1:1, 2)
From: Jerusalem

THE BOOK

Number in Bible	59
Number in N.T.	20
Chapters	5
Verses	108

PURPOSE

To show the conflict between inner and outer man:

Perfection	Inner problems + outer persecution
Excellence	Inner experience + outer exposure
Maturity	Inner misery + outer misunderstanding
Character	Inner conflict + outer conviction
Stability	Inner sorrow + outer suffering

DIVISIONS

The Perfect Man

Patient in testing: chap. 1
Practices the truth: chap. 2
Power over the tongue: chap. 3
Peacemaker, not troublemaker: chap. 4
Prays in trouble: chap. 5

OUTLINE

Introduction: Christ and His Brother: Chapter 1:1

I. A Christian and His Battles: Chapter 1:2–16
  A. His testings: vss. 2–12
  B. His temptations: vss. 13–16
II. A Christian and His Bible: Chapter 1:17–27
  A. Gift of the Word: vss. 17,18
  B. Grafting of the Word: vss. 19–22
  C. Glass of the Word: vss. 23, 24
III. A Christian and His Brethren: Chapter 2:1–13
  A. Partiality: a sin against the Lord: vss. 1–7
  B. Partiality: a sin against the Law: vss. 8–13

IV. A Christian and His Beliefs: Chapter 2:14–26
   A. Faith vs. works: emphatically declared: vss. 14–17
   B. Faith vs. works: energetically debated: vss. 18–20
   C. Faith vs. works: examples delivered: vss. 21–26
V. A Christian and His Behavior: Chapters 3:1–4:12
   A. Sin must be revealed: chaps. 3:1–4:4
   B. Sin must be resisted: chap. 4:5–12
VI. A Christian and His Boasting: Chapters 4:13–5:6
   A. Wrong to boast about his plans: chap. 4:13–17
   B. Wrong to boast about his prosperity: chap. 5:1–6
VII. A Christian and His Burdens: Chapter 5:7–20
   A. Burden of poverty: vs. 7
   B. Burden of proof: vs. 12
   C. Burden of prayer: vss. 13–18
   D. Burden of people: vss. 19, 20

MISCELLANEOUS

Information on the Book of James
   General Epistle
   Called Proverbs of the New Testament
   Probably first book of New Testament written
   Practical guide to Christian life conduct
   Deals with ethics and morals
   Filled with metaphors and figures

CONTRAST

BOOK OF HEBREWS	BOOK OF JAMES
Hebrews is doctrine.	James is about deeds.
Paul lays a foundation.	James builds buildings.
Paul talks about Heaven.	James talks about works.
Paul talks about beliefs.	James talks about behavior.

The half brother of Jesus
Servant of God
Servant of the Lord Jesus Christ
Son of Mary and Joseph
Pillar in the church at Jerusalem
Pastor of the church at Jerusalem
Called "Old Camel Knees"
Thrown to death by Ananias from balcony and stoned

I PETER
Serving in Persecution

KEY VERSE: I Peter 1:7

"That the trial of your faith, being much more precious than of gold that perisheth, though it be tried with fire, might be found unto praise and honour and glory at the appearing of Jesus Christ."

KEY WORD
Forms of "suffer" used 16 times
1st use: chap. 1:11
Most significant use: chap. 3:17

THEME
Grace in time of suffering

DATE
A.D. 63–64 (approximately)

WRITER
Simon Peter

WRITTEN
To: Strangers (Jews in a foreign land) scattered throughout Asia Minor
From: Ephesus probably

THE BOOK
Number in Bible   60
Number in N.T.   21

Chapters   5
Verses   105

PURPOSE
To teach God's truth concerning:
Salvation	chap. 1:5
Holiness	chap. 2:12
Fellowship	chap. 3:8
Grace	chap. 4:10
Glory	chap. 5:4

DIVISIONS
1. Relation to God: chaps. 1:1–2:10
2. Relation to Believer: chaps. 2:11–4:19
3. Relation to Church: chap. 5

OUTLINE
I. The Christian's Lively Hope, and How to React to It
  A. The Living Hope—chap. 1:3–12
    Our reaction to it: chap. 1:13–21
  B. The Living Word—chaps. 1:22–25
    Our responsibility to it: chap. 2:1–3
  C. The Living Stone—chap. 2:4
    Our relation to it: chap. 2:5–10
II. The Christian's Life as a Pilgrim, and How to Live It
In the realm of:
  A. Citizenship: chap. 2:12–17
  B. Servanthood: chap. 2:18–25
  C. Marriage: chap. 3:1–7
III. The Christian's Load of Burden, and How to Bear It
  A. Exceeding joy in times of trials: chap. 4:12–19
  B. Exhortations in times of trials: chap. 5:1–4

C. Examples in times of trials: chap. 5:5–11

MISCELLANEOUS

About the author—Peter

Simon means "hearing."

Barjona means "son of Jonas."

Peter means "little stone." (By hearing our faith becomes like a rock.)

II PETER
Equipped for the Last Days

KEY VERSE: II Peter 1:3

"According as his divine power hath given unto us all things that pertain unto life and godliness, through the knowledge of him that hath called us to glory and virtue."

KEY WORDS

Forms of "know"—used 9 times
   1st use: chap. 1:12
   Most significant use: chap. 2:21
   "Knowledge"—used 7 additional times
   1st use: chap. 1:2
   Most significant use: chap. 3:18

THEME

Believer's responsibility in time of apostasy

DATE

A.D. 67, shortly before Peter's death

WRITER

Simon Peter

WRITTEN

To: Jewish Christians (to be applied to every Christian of every age, everywhere)

From: Ephesus (probably)

THE BOOK

Number in Bible   61

Number in N.T.	22
Chapters	3
Verses	61

PURPOSE

In Peter's first letter, he was writing to encourage the recipients and to hearten them amid persecution and suffering.

He had learned that false teachers among them were teaching false doctrine, so he sent this short letter to remind the readers to ground themselves more firmly in the full knowledge of truth in Christ Jesus and thereby to reinforce their faith against false doctrine.

DIVISIONS

1. Believer's Sure Foundation: Knowledge of Bible: chap. 1
2. Believer's Solemn Warning: Knowledge of Apostates: chap. 2
3. Believer's Satisfying Hope: Knowledge of Second Coming: chap. 3

OUTLINE

I. Knowledge of Bible: Chapter 1

    A. Gift of Knowledge: chap. 1:1–4

        1. Through divine conversion: "Simon Peter": vs. 1

        2. Through divine calling: "apostle": vs. 1

        3. Through divine communion: "like precious faith": vs. 1

        4. Through divine contentment: "peace": vs. 2

        5. Through divine control: "power": vs. 3

        6. Through divine charge: "glory and virtue": vs. 3

        7. Through divine company: "nature": vs. 4

    B. Growth of Knowledge (Add to Your Faith): chap. 1:5–11

1. Separation: "virtue": vs. 5
2. Study: "knowledge": vs. 5
3. Self-Control: "temperance": vs. 6
4. Suffering: "patience": vs. 6
5. Spirituality: "godliness": vs. 6
6. Service: "brotherly kindness": vs. 7
7. Sacrifice: "love": vs. 7

C. Grounded in Knowledge: chap. 1:12–21
1. By what he had seen and heard: vs. 17
2. By what he had studied and heeded: vs. 19
3. By what he had searched and held: vs. 21

II. Knowledge of Apostates: Chapter 2
A. Their Condemnation: chap. 2:1–9
1. The infiltration: "among you": vs. 1
2. The iniquity: "damnable heresies": vs. 1
3. The influence: "many shall follow": vs. 2
4. The insincerity: "feigned words": vs. 3
5. The indictment: "damnation": vs. 3
6. The imprisonment: "reserved": vss. 4
7. The innocent: "godly": vs. 9

B. Their Character: chap. 2:10–16
1. Their self-will and rebellion: vss. 10, 11
2. Their sure judgment and reward: vss. 12, 13
3. Their sinful ways and results: vss. 14–16

C. Their Claims: chap. 2:17–22
1. They promise fullness; they are empty: vss. 17, 18.
2. They promise freedom; they are enslaved: vs. 19.
3. They produce failure; they are excluded: vs. 22.

III. Knowledge of Second Coming: Chapter 3
A. Beloved, "be mindful": vss. 1–7

B. Beloved, "be not ignorant": vss. 8–10
C. Beloved, "be diligent": vss. 11–14
D. Beloved, "beware": vss. 15–18

MISCELLANEOUS
Comparison:

I Peter warns of a roaring lion (persecution from without).

II Peter warns of a deceiving serpent (false teaching from within).

I Peter: The theme is "grace."
II Peter: The theme is "knowledge."

Peter wraps it up in II Peter 3:18 where we are urged to grow in "grace, and…knowledge."

Simon: name given at first birth (speaks of old man)
Peter: name given at new birth (speaks of new man)—
Matt. 16:18

I JOHN

Assurance in Christ

KEY VERSES: I John 5:11–13

"And this is the record, that God hath given to us eternal life, and this life is in his Son.

"He that hath the Son hath life; and he that hath not the Son of God hath not life.

"These things have I written unto you that believe on the name of the Son of God; that ye may know that ye have eternal life, and that ye may believe on the name of the Son of God."

KEY WORDS

Forms of "love"—used 46 times
  1st use: chap. 2:5
  Most significant use: chap. 4:7–11
Forms of "know"—used 38 times
  1st use: chap. 2:3
  Most significant use: chap. 5:13

THEME

Fellowship: fellows in the same ship; fellows in common

DATE

A.D. 90

WRITER

Apostle John

WRITTEN
To: Christians in Asia Minor
From: Ephesus (probably)

THE BOOK
Number in Bible	62
Number in N.T.	23
Chapters	5
Verses	105

PURPOSE
Fourfold Purpose of I John
'I write...'
1. "That your joy may be full": chap. 1:4
2. "That ye sin not": chap. 2:1
3. 'That you might be aware of seducers': chap. 2:26
4. "That ye may know that ye have eternal life": chap. 5:13

DIVISIONS
1. God is Light: Chap. 1, 2.
2. God is Love: Chap. 3, 4.
3. God is Life: Chap. 5.

OUTLINE
Introduction: The Reality of Christ
I. Our Relationship to the Father: Chapter 1
   A. Fellowship with the Father: vs. 3
   B. Fullness of the Father: vs. 4
   C. Faithfulness of the Father: vs. 9
   D. Forgiveness from the Father: vs. 9
II. Our Righteousness and Our Surroundings: Chapter 2
   A. Our righteousness and sin: vs. 1
   B. Our righteousness and His commandments: vs. 3

C. Our righteousness and others: vs. 6

D. Our righteousness and our brother: vss. 9–11

E. Our righteousness and the world: vss. 15, 16

F. Our righteousness and the Holy Spirit: vss. 20–27

III. Our Responsibility to Love One Another: Chapter 3

A. Because of God's pattern: vs. 1

B. Because of the blessed hope: vss. 2, 3

C. Because of His death for us: vss. 4–8

D. Because of our new nature: vss. 9–18

E. Because of the Holy Spirit: vss. 19–24

IV. Our Reaction as a Child of God: Chapter 4

A. We have light in discerning spirits: vss. 1–6.

B. We have love in dealing with others: vss. 7–14.

C. We have loyalty in dedication to the Lord: vss. 15–21.

V. Our Response to the Truth of God: Chapter 5

A. We understand what a Christian is: vss. 1–5.

B. We understand who Christ is: vss. 6–13.

MISCELLANEOUS

Three words about fellowship:

Basis: walking in light: chap. 1:7

Barriers: walking in sin: chap. 1:6

Benefits: fellowship with one another: chap. 1:7

Seven times John uses "as he" or "as he is."

1. Fellowship: "...as he is in the light": chap. 1:7

2. Abiding: "...even as he walked": chap. 2:6

3. Likeness: "...we shall see him as he is": chap. 3:2

4. Purity: "...even as he is pure": chap. 3:3

5. Righteousness: "...even as he is righteous": chap. 3:7

6. Love: "...as he gave us commandment": chap. 3:23

7. Representation: "...as he is, so are we in this world": chap. 4:17

I John, an epistle of certainties: "We know…"
1. A righteous life indicates regeneration: chaps. 2:29; 5:18.
2. We shall be like Christ at His coming: chap. 3:2.
3. Christ came to take away our sins: chap. 3:5.
4. Brotherly love indicates that we have passed from death unto life: chap. 3:14.
5. He abideth in us by the witness of the Spirit: chap. 3:24.
6. We have eternal life: chap. 5:13.
7. Our prayers are answered: chap. 5:15.

John was:
One of the 5,000 fed
One of the 120 in the upper room
One of the twelve apostles
One of three in the inner circle
"The disciple whom Jesus loved"
Banished to the isle of Patmos, ten-by-six-mile rocky island in Aegean Sea, by Roman emperor Domitian.
Only surviving apostle at the time of writing
Called 'the son of thunder'
Son of Zebedee
Pastor at Ephesus from A.D. 70
Wrote John; I, II, III John; Revelation

II JOHN
Discernment

KEY VERSE: II John 8

"Look to yourselves, that we lose not those things which we have wrought, but that we receive a full reward."

KEY WORDS
"Truth"—used 5 times
> 1st use: vs. 1
> Most significant use: vs. 4

"Love"—used 4 times
> 1st use: vs. 1
> Most significant use: vs. 6

THEME
Walk in truth and love

DATE
A.D. 95–98

WRITER
Apostle John, oldest and only surviving apostle; called himself "elder"

WRITTEN
To: A Christian mother and her children; some say Martha, sister of Mary of Bethany. Others say the local church at Ephesus.

"Lady" in Greek is *kuria*. It could be a person or could have reference to the church.

From: Ephesus

Digest of the New Testament ─────────────

THE BOOK

Number in Bible	63
Number in N.T.	24
Chapters	1
Verses	13

PURPOSE

To give this mother a good report about her children and to warn of seducing deceivers teaching false doctrines

DIVISIONS

1. Commendation: walking in truth: vss. 1–4
2. Commandment: "love one another": vss. 5, 6
3. Caution: careful of false doctrine and teachers: vss. 7–11
4. Conclusion: will say more at eye-to-eye meeting: vs. 12

OUTLINE

Introduction

Who is writing?	Vs. 1
To whom is he writing?	Vs. 1
What is he writing about?	Vs. 2

I. Lady Commended: Vs. 4

    A. Satisfaction of the elder

    B. Size of his joy

    C. Surprise element

    D. Scripture

II. Lady Commanded: Vss. 5, 6

    A. To love

    B. To live it

III. Lady Cautioned: Vss. 7–11

    A. Caution among deceivers: vs. 7

    B. Caution about diligence: vs. 8

C. Caution around duty: vs. 11

MISCELLANEOUS

"Full reward" suggests that there are degrees of reward. The New Testament speaks of different crowns that will be awarded.

FIVE DIFFERENT CROWNS	GIVEN FOR	REFERENCE
Incorruptible Crown	Disciplined Life	I Cor. 9:25
Crown of Life	Patience in Endurance	Jas. 1:12
Crown of Rejoicing	Soul Winning	I Thess. 2:19, 20
Crown of Glory	Faithfulness	I Pet. 5:2–4
Crown of Righteousness	Loving His Appearing	II Tim. 4:8

III JOHN
Support for Servants

KEY VERSE: III John 8

"We therefore ought to receive such, that we might be fellowhelpers to the truth."

KEY WORD
"Truth"—used 6 times
1st use: vs. 1
Most significant use: vs. 4

THEME
Truth and love vs. pride and strife

DATE
A.D. 90

WRITER
Apostle John

WRITTEN
To: Gaius (elder in the church)
From: Ephesus

THE BOOK

Number in Bible	64
Number in N.T.	25
Chapters	1
Verses	14

PURPOSE
1. To commend Gaius
2. To warn of Diotrephes
3. To commend Demetrius

DIVISIONS
1. The Concern of John: Vss. 1, 2
2. The Compliment to Gaius: Vss. 3–8
3. The Condemnation of Diotrephes: Vss. 9, 10
4. The Commendation of Demetrius: Vss. 11, 12
5. The Conclusion: Vss. 13, 14

OUTLINE
Introduction
The elder: seasoned saint
Tried and tested, experienced and exposed, seen and heard

I. The Practicing Christian and Prospering: Vss. 1–8
   Gaius
   A. Loved ("beloved" found four times): vss. 1, 2, 5, 11
   B. Prospers: vs. 2
   C. Walks in truth: vss. 3, 4
   D. Faithful in labor: vs. 5
   E. Unselfish: vs. 7

II. The Proud Christian and Problems: Vss. 9–11
   Diotrephes
   A. Proud and self-centered: vs. 9
   B. Critical and slanderous: vs. 10
   C. Lacks concern for the brethren: vs. 10
   D. Influences and hinders others: vs. 10
   E. Wants the preeminence: vs. 9

III. The Pleasant Christian and Praise: Vss. 12–14
   Demetrius
   A. Well spoken of: vs. 12
   B. Possibly turned from worship of Diana: Acts 19:24
   C. Lived in truth: vs. 12

MISCELLANEOUS
   The emphasis of III John is
      1. Sincerity
      2. Hospitality
      3. Christian character

JUDE
Earnestly Contending

KEY VERSE: Jude 3

"Beloved, when I gave all diligence to write unto you of the common salvation, it was needful for me to write unto you, and exhort you that ye should earnestly contend for the faith which was once delivered unto the saints."

KEY WORD
"Ungodly"—used 6 times
1st use: vs. 4
Most significant use: vs. 4

THEME
Contending for the Faith

DATE
A.D. 67–68

WRITER
Jude, half brother of Jesus (see Matt. 13:55; Mark 6:3)

WRITTEN
To: Believers in general ("sanctified," "preserved," "called")
From: Palestine (probably)

THE BOOK
Number in Bible   65
Number in N.T.   26

Chapters   1
Verses   25

PURPOSE
1. To warn against certain false teachers
2. To instruct his readers in the common salvation
3. To urge believers to contend for the Faith

DIVISIONS
1. Those Delivered From Sin: Vs. 1
2. Those Devoted to God: Vss. 2, 3
3. Those Defenders of the Faith: Vss. 4–19
4. Those Determined to Obey: Vss. 20–23
5. Those Desiring to See Christ: Vss. 24, 25

OUTLINE
Introduction: Vss. 1, 2
  I. Why We Contend: Vss. 3, 4
 II. With Whom We Contend: Vss. 5–19
     A. Forerunners of the apostates: vss. 5–7
     B. Disrespect of the apostates: vss. 8–10
     C. Judgment of the apostates: vss. 11–15
     D. Prophecy about the apostates: vss. 16–19
III. How We Contend: Vss. 20–23
     A. Prayer: vs. 20
     B. Righetous Living: vs. 21
     C. Soul Winning: vss. 22, 23
Conclusion: Vss. 24, 25

MISCELLANEOUS
Threefold Lists in Jude

Apostates
1. Attributes: vss. 12, 13
2. Attitudes: vss. 14–18

3. Arrogance: vs. 19

Salvation
1. Mercy: vs. 2
2. Peace: vs. 2
3. Love: vs. 2

Beloved
1. Purpose of writing: vs. 3
2. Prophecy of words: vs. 17
3. Program of walk: vs. 20

Purpose to inform them of
1. Common salvation: vs. 3
2. Contending exhortation: vs. 3
3. Certain men: vs. 4

Relationship
1. Natural
2. Spiritual
3. National

Obligation
1. Having compassion of some: vs. 22
2. Helping others out of fire: vs. 23
3. Hating garment spotted by fire: vs. 23

Reference of Apostasy
1. Unbelieving Israel: vs. 5
2. Uncontrolled angels: vs. 6
3. Ungodly Sodom: vs. 7

Corruption
1. Way of Cain: vs. 11
2. Error of Balaam: vs. 11
3. Gainsaying of Core: vs. 11

Relationship to Faith
1. Contending for Faith: vs. 3
2. Denying the Faith: vs. 4
3. Living by faith: vs. 20

Position
1. Sanctified (saved): vs. 1
2. Preserved (secure): vs. 1
3. Called (surrendered): vs. 1

Signs of Apostasy
1. Defilers of flesh: vs. 8
2. Despisers of dominion: vs. 8
3. Derogatory of dignitaries: vs. 8

Appeal to Build by
1. Praying in Spirit: vs. 20
2. Keeping self in love of God: vs. 21
3. Looking for mercy: vs. 21

Benediction
1. He is able to keep us from falling: vs. 24.
2. He is able to present us faultless: vs. 24.
3. He is the only wise God: vs. 25.

REVELATION
Foreview of Glory

KEY VERSE: Revelation 1:18

"I am he that liveth, and was dead; and, behold, I am alive for evermore, Amen; and have the keys of hell and of death."

KEY WORDS
"I beheld"—used 7 times
    1st use: chap. 5:6
    Most significant use: chap. 5:6
"I saw"—used 35 times
    1st use: 1:12
    Most significant use: chap. 21:1

THEME
Revelation of Jesus Christ
Things which were, are and will be

DATE
A.D. 95–98

WRITER
Apostle John

WRITTEN
To: The seven churches of Asia (Rev. 1:4), the servants of Jesus Christ (Rev. 1:1), and all who will read (Rev. 1:3)
From: Isle of Patmos, off the coast of Asia Minor

THE BOOK
Number in Bible	66
Number in N.T.	27
Chapters	22
Verses	404

PURPOSE
1. To unveil or reveal Jesus Christ
2. To instruct, encourage and rebuke the professing church

DIVISIONS
1. Past	Things That Were	Chap. 1
2. Present	Things That Are	Chaps. 2, 3
3. Future	Things That Will Be	Chaps. 4–22

OUTLINE
I. "The Things Which Thou Hast Seen": Chapter 1
   A. Receiving the inspired message: chap. 1:1–8
   B. Regarding the glorified Christ: chap. 1:9–20
II. "The Things Which Are": Chapters 2–3
   A. The church of Ephesus: chap. 2:1–7
   B. The church of Smyrna: chap. 2:8–11
   C. The church of Pergamos: chap. 2:12–17
   D. The church of Thyatira: chap. 2:18–29
   E. The church of Sardis: chap. 3:1–6
   F. The church of Philadelphia: chap. 3:7–13
   G. The church of Laodicea: chap. 3:14–22
III. "The Things Which Shall Be Hereafter": Chapters 4–22
   A. Seven seals: chaps. 4:1–8:1
   B. Seven trumpets: chaps. 8:2–11:19
   C. Satan and the Antichrist battled: chaps. 12–14
   D. Seven vials: chaps. 15–16

E. Satan and the Antichrist judged: chaps. 17–20

F. New Heaven and earth: chaps. 21–22

MISCELLANEOUS

Comparing Daniel and Revelation
"Seal the book" (Dan. 12:4).
"Seal not the sayings of...this book" (Rev. 22:10).

Rule of interpretation for Revelation:
"When the plain sense makes common sense, seek no other sense."

The Channel
1. God gave the Revelation to Christ.
2. Christ gave the Revelation to an angel.
3. The angel gave the Revelation to John.
4. John gave the Revelation to us.

Christ in the Revelation
I. Christ Among the Seven Candlesticks: Chapter 1:12, 13
II. Christ on the Throne: Chapter 4:10,11
III. Christ in the Midst of 144,000: Chapter 7:4, 17
IV. Christ on the White Horse: Chapter 19:11
V. Christ on the Great White Throne: Chapter 20:11
VI. Christ, the Light of the Holy City: Chapter 21:23
VII. Christ, the Bright and Morning Star: Chapter 22:16

The Four Visions of John

1. Patmos	Son of Man	Christ and Churches	1:9–3:22
2. Heaven	Throne and Lamb	Christ as Lamb	4:2–7:17
3. Wilderness	Woman and Beast	Christ as King	17:1–7
4. Mountain	New Jerusalem	Christ and Bride	21:1–22:5

Genesis and Revelation: The beginnings of Genesis have their fulfillments in Revelation.

Genesis	Revelation
1. Creation of Heaven and Earth: 1:1	New Heaven and New Earth: 21:1
2. Satan's First Attack on Man: 3:1–6	Satan's Final Attack: 20:7–10
3. The Sun to Rule the Day: 1:16	No Need of the Sun: 21:23
4. Darkness and Night: 1:5	No Night There: 22:5
5. The Seas Created: 1:10	No More Sea: 21:1
6. A River in the Garden: 2:10–14	Heavenly River of Life: 22:1, 2
7. Curse Placed on Man and Nature: 3:14–17	No More Curse: 22:3
8. Man Driven Out of Paradise: 3:24	Man Restored to Paradise: 22:11
9. Tree of Life Taken From Man: 3:24	Tree of Life Open to Man: 22:14
10. Nimrod Rebels; Founds Babylon: 10:8–10	Antichrist and Babylon Judged: 17–19
11. Marriage of Adam: 2:18–23	Marriage of the Lamb: 19:6–9
12. The Serpent's Doom Promised: 3:15	The Serpent's Doom Accomplished: 20:10

Four Schools of Interpretation

Preterist	Fulfilled
Historicist	From John to End of World
Futurist	Premillennialist
Spiritual	Symbolic

For a complete list of books available from the Sword of the Lord, write to Sword of the Lord Publishers, P. O. Box 1099, Murfreesboro, Tennessee 37133.

(800) 251-4100
(615) 893-6700
FAX (615) 848-6943
www.swordofthelord.com